The last 2 notes in the left may be omitted if necessary for the page turn.

29
F(add2) F C C Em F(add2)
warm and real and bright, and the world has some - how shift - ed.
L.H.
low G♮
33
R.H. R.H.
L.H.
C G7/C C F G7
All at once, ev - 'ry - thing looks dif - f'rent, now that I see
37
C
you.
41
C G7/C C G7/C C
All those days, chas - ing down a day - dream. All those years liv - ing in a blur.

F C/E F G7 C D7 G7sus G7
All that time, nev - er tru - ly see - ing things the way they were.
low F♯
F♯
low F♮
F♮
C G7/C C G7/C C
Now she's here, shin - ing in the star - light. Now she's here suddenly I know:
F Em7 Am D7 G7sus G7
if she's here, it's crys - tal clear I'm where I'm meant to go. And at
middle F♯
F♯
middle F♮
F♮
Fsus2 F C(add2) G7sus G7 Csus C
last I see the light, and it's like the fog has lift - ed. And at

F(add2) F C(add2)/E C/E E7sus E E/G♯ Am Am/G
last I see the light, and it's like the sky is new. And it's
middle G♯
middle G♮
F C Em7 G/F F(add2)
warm and real and bright, and the world has some - how shift - ed.
R.H.
L.H.
C G7/C C F G7sus C Csus C/B
All at once, ev - 'ry - thing is dif - f'rent, now that I see you.
Am D9 G7sus G7 C C(add2)
Now that I see you.
low F♯
low F♮
F♯
F♮